Spiritual Warfare

*Equipping
yourself
for battle*

PRESENTED BY

Jill Briscoe

NexGen™ is an imprint of
Cook Communications Ministries, Colorado Springs, Colorado 80918
Cook Communications, Paris, Ontario
Kingsway Communications, Eastbourne, England

SPIRITUAL WARFARE
© 2003 by *Just Between Us* magazine

First Printing, 2003
Printed in the United States of America

1 2 3 4 5 6 7 8 9 10 Printing/Year 07 06 05 04 03

This book is part of a series on relevant issues for today's Christian woman.
For more information on other titles in this series or for information about *Just
Between Us* magazine, please turn to the back of this book.

Library of Congress Cataloging-in-Publication Data

Spiritual warfare : equipping yourself for battle / [edited by] Jill Briscoe.
        p. cm. -- (Just between us)
    ISBN 0-7814-3948-5 (pbk.)
    1. Christian women--Religious life. 2. Spiritual warfare. I.
Briscoe, Jill. II. Series.
    BV4527.S654 2003
    248.8'43--dc21

                                                    2003006906

contents

A Note from Jill Briscoe

Dear Friends,

We're living in a war zone, and that's why we've devoted this book to "spiritual warfare." But we who love the Lord have a secret weapon. It must be a "secret weapon" because many Christians don't seem to know about it, or if they do, they don't bother using it. However, it is certainly no secret to the devil. That weapon is prayer. As the little couplet says: "The devil trembles when he sees the weakest saint upon his knees."

The basis of effective prayer is helplessness. When we are in the heat of battle, we must quickly come to "wits' end corner" and cry out to God. It is in prayer that we can talk to God and "complain" about the devil doing his worst to us—and it is in prayer that we will be reminded that Jesus will do His best for us.

When we are on our faces before God, we can confess the sins we have committed that have the devil believing he rules our lives. And then we can take the Sword of the Spirit which is the Word of God (Eph. 6:17) and tell that old serpent, "sin shall not be my master" (Rom. 6:14).

Is the devil using "the world" to make you discontent? Read Phillipians 4:12 and remember "the content of contentment" is Christ. Is the devil using your flesh to bring you down? Are you tempted to be ungrateful to your husband, disloyal to your leaders, or give into sinful appetites? "Resist the devil, and he will flee from you" (James 4:7). In the power of the Holy Spirit, just say no!

As Satan's footsteps dog you, remind him in a loud voice, "God's fingerprints are all over my life, because prayer puts them there." Run to God and don't give up. Always remember the crib, the cross, and the crown, and believe what you believe!

The devil may be allowed to touch everything you have, but God will never allow him to touch anything you are (see Job 1:12). God rules, not Satan. He is the Prince of the power of the air; Jesus is the King of Kings and Lord of Lords, Prince of all Princes.

So make the horrible creature sick to his horrible stomach, and hide in God, and let the Lord finish him off. May we, women in ministry, exhort each other in the immortal words of Corrie ten Boom: "Keep on kicking the devil" or short, KOKD!

Enjoying His Victory,

Jill Briscoe

chapter one

*W*ar
Against the Soul

By becoming aware of the forces that
wage war against your soul,
you'll be better equipped to do battle.

Stuart Briscoe

*B*enjamin Franklin in his famous "Poor Richard's
Almanac" commented that "A little neglect may
breed mischief," and illustrated his point by saying, "For
want of a nail, the shoe was lost, for want of a shoe the
horse was lost, for want of a horse the rider was lost, for
want of a rider the battle was lost, for want of a battle the
kingdom was lost." His aphorism, as well as illustrating
the dangers of a "little neglect," can also be used to
demonstrate that often the great battles are won or lost,
not necessarily because of planning by the generals in
the situation room, but by the effectiveness of the solitary
man guarding his position and fulfilling his role on a
lonely hill.

In recent years great emphasis has been placed on
the fact that human beings live in an environment that is
the scene of a titanic struggle between the forces of good
and evil. Paul taught the Ephesian Christians that they
were not to regard their struggles purely from a human

point of view, but to recognize, "our struggle is not against flesh and blood, but against the rulers, against the authorities, against the powers of this dark world and against the spiritual forces of evil in the heavenly realms" (Eph. 6:12). At the time, Paul was in prison at the mercy of the Emperor, awaiting trial which would eventually lead to his execution in Rome. So while he was struggling with the deprivations, indignities, discomforts, and uncertainties of life in a Roman prison, he saw his struggle as more than that; it was not all about flesh and blood. He recognized he was involved in spiritual warfare.

> ## Life Lifters
> "*The* Devil will let a preacher prepare a sermon if it will keep him from preparing."
> —**Vane Havner**—

Failure to recognize the reality of spiritual warfare by seeing the travails of this life as nothing more than human struggles is as serious as a soldier on the battlefield failing to recognize the enemy and fighting the wrong battle. That leads to defeat. We do well to remember that as long as we inhabit a place in this world, we are living in a war zone, and the forces of evil lined up against us are spiritual and formidable and can only be countered by spiritual dynamics.

An understanding of the scope of the spiritual conflict in which we find ourselves has led to a healthy emphasis on the need to concentrate on the spiritual disciplines and dynamics that will allow us to "be strong in the Lord" in order that we might take our "stand against the devil's schemes," (Eph. 6:11). But it has also led in some instances to emphases that are not always helpful. For example, where there is a great emphasis on the cosmic dimensions of spiritual warfare, there can be a tendency to see everything as the work of the devil through the agency of demons and spirits to the exclusion of other factors. This can lead to a kind of "the devil made me do it" theology which overlooks the fact that the devil can't make you do anything. He's powerful but not that powerful. He doesn't make you do anything; you choose to do it!

Then there is the tendency to see everything from the "situation room" perspective while giving scant regard to the fact that battles are won and lost on the field of conflict, often in the lonely place by the courageous individual. So we must beware of concentrating so much on the identification of "territorial spirits" which may or may not exist, and in taking dramatic measures to "break down strongholds" which may or may not be there, that we overlook the lonely, courageous work of the individual doing battle in the mundane things of life.

Peter was aware of this when he wrote, "Dear friends, I urge you, as aliens and strangers in the world, to abstain from sinful desires, which war against the soul" (1 Peter 2:11). His emphasis was not so much on a great spiritual conflict of cataclysmic proportions between gargantuan forces taking place somewhere out there in the "heavenlies" as on the "war against [the] soul" taking place in the realm of "sinful desires."

"War against the soul" (*psyche* in Greek) refers to the things that go on within the inner recesses of a human being's personality that can lead to the destruction of what that person is intended to be. There is a great conflict "out there" in the heavenlies—

the situation room where the generals strategize and mobilize—but the battle is being fought "in there" where human desires and emotions, aspirations, and phobias reign. What Peter is saying is if we don't handle these things properly, an individual can be rendered spiritually impotent, and a skirmish may be lost in the lonely place. And if our analogy from Franklin's aphorism is valid, for the want of a single rider a much larger battle may be lost. In fact, this is precisely what Peter is concerned about. He wants the people to handle the war against their souls properly in order that they may "live such good lives among the pagans that, though they accuse you of doing wrong, they may see your good deeds and glorify God on the day he visits us," (1 Peter 2:12).

What then are the forces that wage war against the soul? What is it that can so debilitate a believer that she becomes a nonfactor in the struggle for the souls of men and women—or worse than a nonfactor, a negative force that plays into the hands of the enemy of our souls? Surprisingly, Peter speaks of nothing more dramatic than "sinful desires" or "fleshly lusts." While Peter gives no details, Paul is very specific about these inner spiritual dynamics. He lists them as "sexual immorality, impurity and debauchery; idolatry and witchcraft; hatred, discord, jealousy, fits of rage, selfish ambition, dissensions, factions and envy; drunkenness, orgies, and the like" (Gal. 5:19-20). Obviously he was addressing the specific things that he saw manifested in first century culture; and it is possible for us to dismiss the list because we zero in on, for example, "idolatry and witchcraft" and feel confident that we don't have a problem. The reality, of course, is that all of us will find something in the list that describes our own inner "demons" even if it is only in the "and the like;" for we all must accept the fact that, regenerate though we are, our sinful propensities were not eradicated in our new birth, and they continue to "war against the soul."

Peter's admonition is straightforward: "Dear friends, I urge you, as aliens and strangers in the world, to abstain from sinful desires, which war against the soul." He's talking abstinence! Any recovering alcoholic can tell you that abstinence means recognizing a problem, rejecting the problem, building in disciplines to address the problem, and then calling on a "higher power" to assist in abstaining from the problem. Christians can be more specific. They call their inner drives which are forbidden by God, "sin." They abhor sin, and then calling on the power of the indwelling Spirit, they say "no" to sin and apply themselves in the power of the same Spirit to a life of discipline and glad obedience and dependence.

If we may paraphrase Franklin, "for the want of spiritual discipline a character was lost, for want of a character a testimony was lost, for want of a testimony a message was lost, for want of a message a ministry was lost, for want of a ministry a spiritual warfare was lost." We can do better than that. And we must! Peter shows us how!

chapter two

Three Temptations
of Ministry

Keeping your heart out of Satan's clutches.

Jill Briscoe

When Jesus was baptized and led of the Spirit, He went into the desert to find Satan. He dragged Satan from behind his rock and put His heel on him. Satan was not stalking Jesus; Jesus was stalking Satan. Jesus wanted us to know He'd overcome the enemy and temptation. There have been days in ministry when I needed to know that.

When I married my husband, Stuart, he was not a pastor. Only later did he abandon his first career for ministry. Now, after more than thirty-five years as a ministry spouse, I can say it's tough not to lose heart in ministry. Satan is after our hearts, our ministries, and our marriages. He is, to be blunt, after us.

Saying the hard things about ministry is like a preacher's mentioning divorce at a wedding. We want to think of positive things: "better … richer … health." But it can be beneficial for the bride and groom to hear surprising words—even negative words—that they themselves speak: "worse … poorer … sickness … death." It can be a positive thing to talk of negatives.

In that light, I'd like to discuss three temptations we face in Christian ministry. In His ministry, Jesus faced temptation in three general areas: His legitimate needs, His spiritual gifting, and His personal worship. I've learned to face my temptations in ministry by looking at how Jesus dealt with His.

The Temptation in Legitimate Needs

Food is a valid need, but for forty days and nights, led by the Spirit, Jesus went hungry. Satan had a suggestion: "If you're the Son of God, command these stones to become bread."

Food is a legitimate physical need, but God hadn't provided any for Jesus in that place at that time. The question: would Jesus accept the will of His Father that this was a period of privation designed for His spiritual profit, or would He take matters into His own hands and use His own powers to meet His needs?

Shelter also is a legitimate need, but on many nights, the only roof Jesus had over His head was the stars He had made.

Relationships are a legitimate need. Yet Jesus was lonely—it's lonely at the top—and often went into the desert alone.

It's tempting to lose heart when our legitimate needs aren't met. Some Christians believe God will never allow our needs to go unmet. Yet, when God dictated it, Jesus lived with some unmet needs.

For ten years God called Stuart and me to a place in ministry where we received an inadequate salary. Many of my legitimate needs weren't met. Many of our children's legitimate needs weren't met.

It was tempting, as Jesus was tempted, to take

matters into our own hands and resign from that mission position. But we had to answer the question: Would we accept a period of privation as our Father's will? Could we see that He wanted us to depend upon Him so that we might benefit and grow spiritually? Could we see that lean times can be part of His kingdom plan? We finally came to the conclusion that until God led us out as surely as He had led us in, we were to stay put.

If God leads us like this, we have to face the question, "Do we know how to be poor?"

"Of course," we say. "We were seminary students."

But what if we are called to remain poor? Do we know how not to lose heart then? Poverty can become extremely wearing, especially on the spouse who carries incredible stress taking care of young children. It's hard to live on food stamps. It's hard to put your kids in Head Start when other ministry families can afford nursery school.

> ### Life Lifters
>
> "*Much* of the misery of being in a battle is thinking that we are alone in it ... but you can be sure that the Lord will be with you and help you stand against whatever opposes you."
>
> (Daniel 6:10)
>
> —**Stormie Omartian**—

I remember how hard it was for my husband, who wanted to provide better for his family. I remember his pacing up and down our tiny mission house saying, "If only I'd stayed at the bank." We couldn't get our kids' teeth fixed. We lived in other people's clothes, hand-me-downs. It's tough never to have enough.

I desperately wanted a musical instrument for our youth work, so I put an advertisement in the paper. A kind lady who had a lot of money called me. I thought, I'm going to get my piano, and got so excited. She said, "I just got a new piano. Would you like our old one?"

In that instant, something happened to me. I said, "No, I'd like your new one."

I didn't get either piano, which serves me right, I guess. But I had gotten fed up with God's work getting the old piano. Those are the times we can lose heart.

When we're deprived of legitimate needs, we have to live by every word that proceeds out of the mouth of God. At such times, all we can do is remain focused on God, fixed in His Word, and full of the Spirit.

I think the temptation not to do this becomes strongest when we see ministry affect our families. I remember being 3,000 miles away from our parents, who were dying of different diseases. We didn't have the money to get in a plane and visit as often as we needed to. When my mother-in-law came to visit, she discovered one of the many cancers that eventually took her life. She had little money, no insurance, and no one to look after her at home. We had just arrived from England, so we had no money. We entered eighteen months of cancer surgery, chemotherapy, and medical care with no resources. We nearly lost heart.

When our legitimate needs are not met, we find ourselves tempted to abandon our call to ministry, to escape the time of privation. It is necessary for us to hang in there on the Word of God.

The Temptation in Spiritual Gifting

The second kind of temptation for Christian leaders comes in our spiritual gifting. Satan tempted Jesus to use His gifts "for self-aggrandizement," as John Stott puts it. Satan tempts us in the same way, and the greater our gifts, the more Satan has to work with. He'll say, "Do something mega. Use your abilities to get the crowd. Throw yourself around the temple. Make a splash."

When we get it right and do our best, our gifting can become a snare. John Stott says that a pulpit is a dangerous place for any person, because there we can lose our heart's focus. We can, for example, learn techniques and hone skills that allow us to speak powerfully, yet apart from the Holy Spirit. That's scary! It is possible as G. Campbell Morgan wrote, to be "homiletically brilliant, verbally fluent, theologically profound, biblically orthodox, and spiritually useless." If we focus on our gifts—homiletical ability or theological accuracy—instead of the Giver, God may say, "Preach on, great preacher, but preach without me."

Yes, through my spiritual giftings I can give a solid speech, a nice sermon, and a good word. But will it change people? Will marriages be mended? Will demons be cast out? Will God's kingdom come?

Only if I resist the temptation to use my gifts to do something big, to make a show, to build a name for myself. Our words must worship God before they can go out into our world and make a difference.

Some years ago I was asked to write a daily devotional book. I thought, *This will be easy. I already write in my journal. I can do that without taking time out from my other commitments.* At the end of the year, I figured, I could just take my daily prayer diary and have an instant devotional book. At the end of the year, however, I found I was only a quarter of a way through the book. That experience taught me two things: I wasn't daily, and I wasn't devotional.

It took me two-and-a-half years to complete that daily devotional. At the end of that time, I wrote this in the front:

> Give my words wings, Lord.
> May they alight gently
> on the branches of men's minds,
> bending them to the winds of your will.
> Give my words wings, Lord.
> May they fly high enough to reach the lofty,
> low enough to breathe the breath
> of sweet encouragement
> upon the downcast soul.
> Give my words wings, Lord.
> May they fly swift and far,
> winning the race with the worldly-wise
> to the hearts of men.
> Give my words wings, Lord.
> See them now nesting down at your feet,
> silenced into ecstasy,
> home at last.

I learned that unless my words have worshiped, they will never win the race with the words of the world.

But if Satan can tempt us through the expression of our spiritual gifting, he can also tempt us through the limitation of that same gifting. Sometimes we may be called to serve in a work that is well below our abilities. Then our giftedness can lead to frustrations that make us lose heart.

Before entering ministry, my husband was a bank inspector. At age twenty-five, thanks to his photographic memory, he was assistant to the chief inspector in a British bank. He was offered a world of opportunities in that profession. But then he was called to a mission that had old-fashioned typewriters and sometimes an untrained staff. Their hearts were right, but the resources weren't there.

I saw a poster about that time above a mission secretary's desk: "We, the unwilling, led by the unknowing, are doing the impossible for the ungrateful. We have done so much for so long with so little, we are now qualified to do anything with nothing." That pretty well described our situation.

In such settings, we may feel frustrations that our gifts are underutilized. Then we will be tempted to prove our abilities, to show our stuff. We will feel swayed by the expectations of people around us. People expected Jesus to teach a certain way, to behave a certain way, to wave His miracle wand, to prove His points, to build His empire. Yet Jesus came, according to Isaiah 53, to be unspectacular and unhysterical, not to raise His voice in the streets, to refuse to publish His miracles.

Stuart and I know what it's like to serve in a mega-church, with its own set of temptations, and I've learned that if God calls us to a mega-ministry, we need to pray for a mini-mindset, or we'll end up a mega-nuisance to God's kingdom.

The Temptation in Personal Worship

When Satan came out from behind his rock, stamped his foot, and shouted to Jesus, "Worship me!" Jesus faced His enemy and overcame temptation.

This third temptation is the hardest, I think. It's that power encounter, no-holds-barred, when Satan comes and demands: "Stop worshiping God and start worshiping me." He begins with the direct attack, tempting us to link into any power other than that of the Holy Spirit. Then he asks us to worship him: "Ask me for anything, and I will give it to you."

I don't think Satan has ever come to me that directly until recently. I had fallen into a trap, ordering a catalog of merchandise advertised on the television. A yogurt machine was offered in this little booklet as a prize, so I sent in a little slip and I won! Then, when the little booklet came back, there was a prize offer for a toaster. Since mine had just died, I sent in the little slip and I won! Without giving any money, I won five things straight.

Then one day, shortly after we had appealed for funds to build a new sanctuary, I drove into our church parking lot, which sat next to the building site. Suddenly Satan was right there in the car with me, and he said, "Ask me. Ask me, Jill. I'll give it to you. I'll give you the million dollars."

In that still, horrible moment, I knew he'd come out from behind his rock and said, "Worship me. Just for a minute. Just see if I can do it." That's what he said to Jesus.

Satan comes with many kinds of offers, including offers of money, sex, and power, to interfere with the things of God's kingdom. Satan has the ability to give such things.

One of the strongest and most alluring offers is the temptation for illicit sexual pleasures. Satan says, "Be queen for a day. Be king for a day. I'll give it to you."

"We need to stop allowing fear to motivate us in this area. It so often seems like whenever Spiritual Warfare is mentioned, we change the subject or look the other way. Satan has too often succeeded in getting us to think that if we so much as study the subject, something awful may happen to us. The opposite is true. The more we know about our victory in Christ, and the more we know about our defeated enemy the more confident we will be in the conflict in which we are engaged and which we cannot avoid."

—Timothy Warner—

I once described sexual temptation that way while speaking at a conference for pastors and their spouses. I spent the rest of that conference counseling people who, since going into ministry, had bought the lie and lived as king or queen for a day.

One young wife said to me, "I never thought it was possible that I could do this. It happened while my husband was in seminary. He still doesn't know. Should I tell him?"

Another extremely pretty woman said, "I thought I could never do that. Then this man came to live next door, and my husband was traveling for the mission, and I was very lonely."

I said, "Like Bathsheba?"

"Yes, like Bathsheba," she said. And when I met King David, I fell."

She lost heart, her husband lost heart, and their marriage fell apart. Today they're out of the ministry.

In these three areas of temptation, Satan's strategy is basic. He simply wanted to stop Jesus from doing the things the Father had sent Him to do. Satan wanted to prevent Jesus from being the obedient, suffering Servant, with His heart focused on the Father, fixed in the Word, and filled with the Spirit.

Satan's devices haven't changed. I believe the more we try to be like Jesus and focus on God, the more we try to be holy, the more Satan will focus on us.

The role of a minister can be hard, as can the role of a minister's spouse. And yet, the One who overcame Satan's temptations is the One who can give us heart. He never lost heart, even though He hung from the cross. That's why He can offer His heart to us. Paul, who knew all about hardship and stress, said, "Since … we have this ministry, we do not lose heart" (2 Cor. 4:1).

If we stay focused on the Father, fixed in the Word, and full of the Spirit, we will be able to face hard times and overcome temptation. We will not lose heart.

chapter three

Armed for
Battle

Protecting your heart, mind,
and soul from the enemy.

Patty Stump

*D*uring the course of my growing-up years, television broadcasts brought into our home various reports and visual images of wars that mostly took place on foreign soil. Many of us can recall the vivid photographs contained in *LIFE* magazine—pictures that captured the victories and viciousness, captives and casualties that resulted from ensuing battles. While these wars were real, they didn't touch my life very deeply. They were events that happened to someone else, somewhere else.

Over the years, I continue to catch glimpses of war, of battles that deeply impact the lives of those they touch—often immobilizing or eliminating faithful soldiers from the front lines of service. I've never served in an official military capacity, yet I've discovered as a Christian that each day we serve on the front lines of a different type of battlefield—the battlefield that hosts the war that rages between those seeking to live as victorious Christians and the illusive enemy who fervently seeks to eliminate his opponents. What is this battle over? Throughout Scripture we see that the battle is for the hearts and minds of those who seek to serve the Lord. And who is the enemy? Ephesians 6:12 informs us that we wrestle against the powers, principalities, and rulers of darkness—namely Satan.

While most of us as Christians would like to settle into the "warm fuzzies" of a comfortable Christian walk, the truth is that if we are seeking to serve the Lord wholeheartedly, we will indeed encounter battles designed to place us on the casualty list. Because we're all different, your battle may occur in a different area of life than mine; but I would venture to guess that the war is waged in a similar fashion, for in the life of each Christian, there are three main areas that are under greatest attack: the battle for the heart, for the mind, and for the soul.

From the outpouring of one's heart, the Lord is able to draw others unto Himself. It comes as no surprise then that a foundational area of attack is on the heart, to harden the heart so that little or nothing pours forth. Bitterness, unresolved hurt, envy, jealousy, and unconfessed sin each play a part in waging war against the heart. These issues allow the enemy opportunities to creep in. Before we know it, our once supple heart becomes calloused and insensitive, cynical and reserved, less inclined to trust in God or to care for others. How can the Lord reach others through us if our hearts are hardened, occupied with bitterness, or cluttered with unresolved issues?

In addition to the battle for the heart there is the war that rages for the mind of the Christian. Romans 12:2 states that as we think within ourselves, so we are. The mind is profoundly influenced by what it takes in. Words spoken by family, friends, or significant others may bring with them wounds that impair us, resulting in a battle against the enemies of self-doubt, worthlessness, shame, or insignificance. Things we set before our eyes are captured within our mind as well. Images or thoughts that are impure and ungodly tend to take root, waging war within the private recesses of our minds. Over time, as the mind becomes clouded regarding the truths of God, the believer is unable to see with clarity or understand with accuracy the call and character of Christ in his or her life.

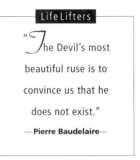

LifeLifters

"*The Devil's most beautiful ruse is to convince us that he does not exist.*"

—Pierre Baudelaire—

Lastly is the battle for the soul. As a Christian, it can be easy to "talk a good talk"; but the truth of our walk lies in what we treasure most deeply within our souls. For Christ to be on the throne of our hearts requires putting Him first above all else. Often the battle for our time crowds out our quiet moments with Christ, leaving us defenseless when trials and times of battle come upon us. If our priorities aren't adjusted, we in turn become lukewarm, limited in our effectiveness for affecting those around us for the Lord.

It has been said that God can use life's setbacks to move us ahead. Indeed, He can work in our lives amidst these various battlefields to strengthen us for the service at hand. Like the tuning of guitar strings, slight adjustments can make a big difference. In order to be victorious in our walk, able to withstand the battles that come our way, we must first let Christ take precedence at the heart of our lives. Practical steps include spending a few quality moments with Him each day through time in His Word, prayer, and journaling. Familiarity with the Lord often breeds complacency; yet if we are to be fruitful in our walk, we must be faithful in our walk.

A second step is to tend to any unfinished business. Confess any sins that stand between you and the Lord. Commit yourself to working through unresolved hurts and issues within your own heart, or conflicts that have occurred between you and another person. Romans 12:18 exhorts us to be at peace with all men as much as is possible within our own abilities.

Finally, be careful what you place before your eyes and into your mind. As we open ourselves up to unwholesome images or information, we create an atmosphere within the mind that invites a battle for our thoughts. Philippians 4:8 instructs us to meditate on things that are true, honest, just, pure, lovely, and of good repute. A mind is a terrible thing to waste!

Battles will occur within the life of every Christian. As we seek to walk upright before the Lord, the silent enemies of our life will seek to deter or destroy our walk of faithfulness. Yet the Lord promises in Philippians 4:13 that we can do everything through Him who strengthens us. Stand firm, be faithful, and stay focused. Keep your gaze upon Him in order that you may be able to run the race that He unfolds before you!

chapter four

Never Say
Never

Shelly Esser

$\mathcal{T}$he student body began filing into the empty conference center for the last time. Bible school was coming to a close. In a matter of hours the international conglomerate of students would say good-bye for the last time, scattering across the globe for home. Finding his way to the podium, our beloved principal looked out at the sea of eager faces to deliver his parting words. With one of the most serious tones he had ever used, he issued this warning: "Never say never. Some of you are going to be shocked at the things you do after leaving Bible school."

It has been a little over a decade since I heard that warning, but I have never forgotten those piercing words. Have you ever noticed how easy it is to become too overconfident, too self-reliant in the Christian life, especially once you've achieved spiritual leadership? We can feel so strong, thinking we can withstand any pressure, any temptation, go anywhere, do anything. However, it's not long before we fall into the trap of our own naïve pride. Proverbs 16:18 says,

"Pride goes before destruction, a haughty spirit before a fall." It is pride that says I will never do this or that.

For years I had this neat little list that I kept tucked away in my spiritual pocket. It went something like this: "I will never commit adultery … I will never divorce my husband … I will never walk away from God … I will never …" and on and on it went. I felt rather smug about my list, feeling like I was above the so-called "big" sins. By saying ever so proudly that we are exempt to any sin is to live in denial and to give a challenge to the enemy for which we are no match. We do not know the circumstances that will send us answering temptation's door. I'm sure David never thought he'd commit adultery or murder. But one day, there was Bathsheba. And Peter, on the eve of Christ's crucifixion, said he would never betray Jesus. But we all know the end of the story. Peter not only betrayed Jesus, he did it three times.

> ### LifeLifters
> "*K*eep me as the apple of Your eye; hide me under the shadow of Your wings, from the wicked who oppress, from my deadly enemies who surround me."
> —**Psalm 17:8-9 (NKJV)**—

It was the great apostle Paul who said in Romans 7:15, "I do not understand what I do. For what I want to do I do not do, but what I hate I do." Matthew 26:41 reminds us that "the spirit is willing, but the flesh is weak" (NASB). Like David and Peter, when we become out of touch with who we are and our own susceptibility to sin, we are more likely to fall into temptation. So often we believe that serious sin is not even a remote possibility for us, underestimating the potential we have for sin in our lives and overestimating our spirituality.

The first step in successfully dealing with temptations that invade our lives is to be honest with ourselves and to believe that we are capable of all our sinful nature longs to do. As we begin to know weak areas, we can begin to watch ourselves. Jill Briscoe in her book, *Prime Rib and Apple* said, "To know yourself is to grow in humility, and to grow in humility is to grow in dependence on God and to grow in dependence on God is to lock and bar the door against Temptation."

Part of knowing ourselves is knowing when the enemy is most likely to strike, and he usually does so at our most vulnerable moments. Jesus encountered temptation right on the heels of a magnificent event in His life: His baptism. Satan is often most dangerous when we think we've made some progress in the Christian life, when we've done something right, something we know has pleased God, when we're on the mountaintop.

As Christian leaders a vulnerable moment might occur after we've received praise from someone about how a song we sang or an article we wrote, or a message our husband delivered blessed them. Or it might occur after we've experienced some victory in the Christian life. Before long we can begin comparing ourselves to others, subtly leading us down the road to pride and overconfidence.

Another time when we are most vulnerable to temptation's invitation is in the wilderness. Satan waited until Jesus was weak in the wilderness to tempt

Him. For the past several years my husband and I have been living in the wilderness. Still in ministry transition, still recovering from past ministry wounds, I have found myself facing temptations that I thought I would never face—much less entertain. I have been deeply sobered by my own vulnerability to sin and the condition of my own heart apart from God's grace and power, realizing that at any moment I am at the edge of the cliff ready to fall into sin.

Scripture tells us that we are to "stand firm" in the face of temptation. "Standing firm" means avoiding the trap of thinking we could never fall prey to the "big" sins. A wise person prepares for those things that are inevitable in life. And James 1:13 tells us that temptation is one of those inevitable things. This is where the body of Christ can really help us out, if we let them. Let's face it, picking up the phone and telling a friend that we're struggling in our thought life or marriage isn't something we're accustomed to doing. But we desperately need to share our sin struggles with others so they can help us stand firm, by praying for us and keeping us accountable. Especially as I have been wandering in the wilderness, I have relied on a few such friends who have greatly assisted me as temptation has relentlessly continued to knock at my door.

Temptation also strikes us in the midst of the hurts in our lives. I can only imagine the types of temptations Jesus wrestled with as He stood before Herod, the chief priests, and the teachers of the law when they vehemently accused, ridiculed, and mocked Him. Yet there He stood in complete silence. He didn't shout back, He didn't try to redeem Himself, He didn't seek revenge. Especially when we are hurt in ministry—by our fellow brothers and sisters in Christ, our teammates or staff members—there is a great temptation to strike back, to become bitter, to quit. By knowing our vulnerabilities during these times, we can arm ourselves with God's Word and respond like Jesus did, in silent love and trust rather than in anger and bitterness.

To win the battle with temptation we must recognize how desperately we need to keep our intimate relationship with Christ alive and growing day by day. It is our intimacy with God that will ultimately play the key role in our ability to keep from falling. This means regularly spending time in His Word and prayer, the very weapons that are ours in the face of battle. Remaining close to God's heart and letting Him regularly examine our lives will give us what we need to resist temptation's invitation time and time again.

A number of years ago, after several Christian leaders fell into sin, singer Sheila Walsh penned the words to the song "It Could Have Been Me." As you read the words, may your eyes be opened to the reality that unless you remain humbly close to Jesus, next time it could be you who loses your grip and falls. But as you read the words, remember the powerful promise of 1 John 4:4, "The one who is in you is greater than the one who is in the world."

It Could Have Been Me

I heard in the news today that another soldier
    stumbled,
A fragile warrior slipped and fell from grace.
The vultures swooped to tear his heart
And pin him to the ground

And from the shadows someone took his place.
Today we'll talk amongst ourselves,
We never bought his words.
We'll say we saw the madness in his eye.
Tomorrow he's forgotten as we've scrubbed him
    from our hearts
And as he bleeds we slowly turn our eyes.

And in our hearts we fear the ones whose lives
    are like our own,
Whose shadows dance like demons in our minds.
We think to push them far away
We'll exorcise our souls.
We'll make them play the tune for all mankind.

But it could have been me.
I could have been the one to lose my grip and fall.
It could have been me,
The one who takes pride in always standing tall.
For unless you hold me tightly, Lord, and I can
    hold on, too,
Then tomorrow in the news it could be me.

(Sheila Walsh, Holding On To Heaven With Hell On Your Back *(Nashville: Thomas Nelson Publishers,* © 1990), p. 137.

There's a Snake in
My Garden

Something was lurking around in the garden of my
ministry marriage—and I didn't like it.

Jill Briscoe

Editor's Note: *With compassion and wit, Jill
Briscoe tells the story of her early life in ministry in her
book,* There's A Snake in My Garden. *In this excerpt,
Jill describes the beginning days of her marriage to
Stuart Briscoe, who had just begun a ministry as a
traveling evangelist. She was anticipating newlywed
bliss, but you'll soon see that instead she hears the
unmistakable hiss of the "snake," twisting Scripture
and tempting her, as he has each one of us, since that
fateful day in the first garden.*

*M*arriage, being God's idea, had to be good! Perhaps it was because marriage was His idea that
He accepted in the person of Jesus Christ the invitation to
the wedding at Cana in Galilee that we read about in John
2. As I wrote our wedding invitations to our relatives and
friends, I sent one to heaven straight from my heart. It
read, "The future Mr. and Mrs. D. S. Briscoe request the
pleasure of the company of Jesus Christ at their wedding."
I had an instant reply by airmail, "Delighted to accept!"

He was coming! How exciting! What would He do? Well—nothing—if He wasn't asked. I knew that from the Scriptures. The problem with the marriage at Cana seemed to be that He was invited as a mere guest, not as governor of the feast. The governor was the one who was in control, gave the orders, and was obeyed. I didn't want Christ to be a guest on the same level as my loved ones and friends—there merely to add a bit of religion to the scene. I did not want the wine of our love to run out nor our relationship to become insipid, colorless, and tasteless. I knew the secret lay in His preeminence as governor and our obedience to His commands. "Whatsoever he saith unto you, do it" (John 2:5, KJV), was the best wedding advice we'd heard anywhere. How foolish of us to buck the divine principles and do our own thing when the Bible taught that our joy (through obedience) would be better than anything we had experienced in our relationship before.

Now I discovered that the snake was still in my garden! Never did I expect him to turn up as consistently as he did in our early days of married bliss! The snake hates any marriage that has the Lord God in control, walking and talking in the cool of the day with the two He made especially for each other and for Himself. God placed man in an ideal environment, but even in Paradise something was missing. "It is not good that the man should be alone," said God (Gen. 2:18, NASB); so He set "the solitary in families" (Ps. 68:6, NKJV), and He started in Eden.

The first hissing suggestion I heard from the snake, as I happily washed, cooked, worked, and cared for our baby David in those early years of marriage, was the usual misquoting of Scripture for which the snake is renowned. Because it sounded familiar to me, I was taken off guard.

"It is not good for man to be alone," he hissed in my ear. "God never intended it, so why does that Christian husband leave you alone so much? He should be here to help you with the baby and the work instead of being busy with God's business!" Next time you hear the hiss of the snake, check up on his quote. I didn't. If I had, I would have remembered that the verse about being alone referred to the man and that the woman was created to help the man, not vice versa.

> ## LifeLifters
>
> "... *The* reason the Son of God appeared was to destroy the devil's work."
>
> —1 **John 3:8**—

The fruit of self-pity looked good to me, so I ate it. It immediately created a desire in me to encourage my husband to eat it also.

"Why don't you stay home on the weekends and evangelize here?" I asked him. "Look over there outside that Cat's Whisker coffee bar across the street. All those young people need to hear the Gospel. Why preach to a dozen little old ladies in church?"

Now let me assure you—I couldn't have cared less about the needy young people across the street. I was simply using them as an excuse to get my own way. I was lonely, and so I was manipulating to get Stuart to obey me rather than God. And I was using a religious excuse to accomplish my purpose. How true is the Scripture that says, "The heart is deceitful above all things, and desperately wicked" (Jer. 17:9, NKJV).

Looking out of our windows and across the street, my husband commented simply, "What do you think you are here for? You reach them."

A thousand excuses leapt to my lips. "My job is to be your wife and look after you and the baby while praying and supporting your ministry. I haven't time!"

"Well, you've more time than I have," he replied. "Jill, God doesn't ask you for your husband's time, or your child's time; He asks you for your spare time!" And with this he packed his case and was gone!

"Well," said the snake, "how unfair. Anyway, you can't go over there and talk to them. They're another generation. (I was twenty-three years old!) Get some teens to go!" This last was said with a smug hiss, as he knew the only Christians I'd met were very young in Christ, shy, and nervous. Of course he'd forgotten the principle of 1 Corinthians 1:26-28, and therefore made a bad mistake.

Seeing a way out of my involvement, I accepted Stuart's advice and decided to invite three or four young people to do those things I didn't dare to do. I would stay home and pray for them (nice of me!) and make an English cup of tea (which is what you always do in times of crisis) in case they needed to retire from the battlefield to recuperate.

The Lord was about to teach me a lesson. God leaned out of heaven and said to me, "Jill, you're right. It is not good for man to be alone or woman for that matter, especially if the man is called away to be about his Father's business. I'm about to rectify the matter and send you some company!" As my three brave but quaking teens went across the road to approach dozens of wild-looking youngsters outside the coffee bar, the establishment closed because of a fight; my three well-trained evangelists panicked and invited everyone back across the street for a free cup of English tea! Looking out of what I had believed was my safe little cocoon, I discovered with horror that the time had come for me to become a butterfly!

"There you are, Jill. We brought them!" my evangelists announced triumphantly. The kids streamed into the house filling every room, chattering and kidding.

"Yes, you did!" I replied weakly. I heard the Lord chuckle. I'm sure it was the Lord. I knew it wasn't the snake as he wasn't in the mood for laughter! Late into the night we talked and witnessed and argued and prayed. Very near midnight my husband returned from his preaching engagement, tried to get in, and couldn't! Hearing Stuart's knock, a lanky youth with hair dyed in different colored strips opened the door a crack and muttered, "Sorry, mate, there's no room!"

It was a new beginning for both of us. My spare time bulged with positive activity, while Stuart fought his own battles with his heart about his involvement with the teens. I sat down and made a note of my daily routine and blocked off my spare time, setting it aside for God. Young people were finding Christ, and follow-up Bible studies began in our home. I thought back to our beautiful wedding service and the text a preacher had spoken from: "It was noised abroad that Jesus was in the house." So it began to be, and the crowds came until, like the Bible story, they could hardly get near Him because of the "press." I prayed, "Oh my Lord, may Your presence in our home be 'news' around town!"

I came to realize that even though I had committed my life to Stuart, this did not mean I had committed my relationship with God to Stuart! That was still my responsibility. Even though we could read and pray and learn of Him together, even though God had a special plan for our lives collectively, I needed to fulfill His plan for my life individually! I needed to guard my own personal devotional time and not let collective devotions take that place. God had work for me to do—spiritual work in areas that my husband never would have had time or talent for.

Our home could be my fishing boat during his absence. Our baby could be a means of contact among other young mothers in the park or at the store. I had a commission from God not only to care physically and practically for my family's needs in a manner that would bring glory to Him, but also to bring the Gospel to every creature. I must not abdicate that responsibility just because I had gotten married!

So many legitimate excuses to fade off the spiritual scene were available in those happy days. As Martha, I was careful and troubled about good and necessary things, but I needed to remember Mary's better part —to sit at His feet and look in His face and listen to His Word. And when I did that, I was continually reminded that two people made one must equal twice the impact for His Kingdom! As God's Word says, "One [of you will] chase a thousand, or two put ten thousand to flight" (Deut. 32:30).

Reprint from There's A Snake in My Garden *by Jill Briscoe (Harold Shaw Publishers) Colorado Springs, CO © 1996. Used by permission.*

The Face of
Spiritual Warfare

Compiled by Shelly Esser

In an effort to give you a close-up of what spiritual warfare looks like in modern-day life, four women—two missionaries, a pastor's wife, and a woman in leadership—candidly share very different personal experiences with spiritual warfare in their own lives, and how they have successfully battled against the attacks of their unseen enemy.

A Mission Field Encounter
Jean Robinson
Veteran Missionary

*I*t was one of those beautiful moonlit nights in the very center of Africa, when the stars shine so bright that you feel as if you could reach out and touch them. The girls in the mission boarding home were having a sleep-out in the middle of their compound; and like all young girls everywhere, they talked long into the hours of the night.

Nearby a very young, inexperienced missionary woman slept soundly in her house. Suddenly she was awakened by a voice calling for her to come quickly to deal with an emergency in the girls' compound. Throwing on a robe, she followed the caretaker down the path to see what the problem was. She came upon a scene like one out of the Bible. A young girl was thrashing around on the ground with super-human strength, yelling out obscenities with a voice not her own. It took the combined strength of all of the other girls to pin her down and keep her from throwing herself into the fire.

I was that young missionary who had been called to help out in this situation. Never did I feel more helpless. I realized that this was a battle, not with flesh and blood but against the powers of darkness of this world, the spiritual forces of evil in the heavenlies. My heart cried out to the Lord for His help. He reminded me of something one of my professors at Bible school had said: "After you get out to the mission field, and when (not if) you encounter *spiritual warfare* in one form or another ... remember that while *you* are weak and powerless, all authority in heaven and earth has been given to Christ. You can claim *His* authority and the power of *His* name and blood over the evil forces."

So, that is what I did. I remember praying for that girl, and claiming the power of Christ's name and blood for deliverance for her. As I did, she let out a horrible scream as the demon left her body, and then she fell into a deep, child-like sleep. Then, sometime later, that girl told me the history of her family. For many generations they had been Satan worshipers and had given themselves to demonic forces to be at work in and through them. The deliverance was a wonderful demonstration of the power of God that is always at our disposal. It was a good lesson for me to learn at the very beginning of my missionary career.

Later on, I worked among people who had been worshippers of the spirit-world. They were especially fearful of evil spirits. A large granite rock stood in the center of the area we lived in. This was the home of the much-feared "spirit of the rain." It was next to this rock that the pioneer missionaries chose to build the mission station of Adi as the base for getting the Gospel out among the Kakwa tribe.The Africans were appalled! Didn't these white people know that if they desecrated that rock, the spirit of the rock would withhold the rains from all of the surrounding area, causing a widespread famine? It had been on that rock that the Kakwa people offered sacrifices to the rain-spirit, and even lacerated their own bodies, causing their blood to flow, to appease him. He was not one to be trifled with! They would watch the white people very closely and fearfully.

And so those pioneers of the Gospel met on that rock, and prayed that the true God would break through the powers of darkness, and that the light of the Gospel would someday shine brightly from that center to all the area around them. When I lived there at Adi, we would walk to that rock on Easter Sunday (together with hundreds of our Kakwa brothers and sisters in Christ) and praise Him for His resurrection power that had set us free from the power of sin and the fear of death.

But Satan didn't give up his hold on that area or those people easily. During the ensuing years of my life in Africa, I was confronted with spiritual warfare in one form or another. While not quite as dramatic as my first encounter, the situations were nevertheless always *very* intense. I felt the onslaught of the evil one in many different ways. Always his goal was to hinder the spread of the Gospel.

Some of the ways Satan attacked included:

• Continued spirit worship, practice, and fears on the part of many of the people.

• Civil war, rebellion, slaughter, and evacuations, such as is going on in the Congo today.

• Many personal encounters with drunken soldiers and their guns along the roads and pathways.

• Border and travel difficulties through Idi Amin's territory in Uganda at the height of his reign and power.

• Life-threatening illnesses that attacked my family members and myself with no medical help nearby.

• The sudden death of my husband.

But through it all, I found Christ's grace, strength, power and victory to be sufficient.

Thank God we don't have to fight these battles alone, but victory is ours through Jesus Christ, as we put on the whole armor of God, each part of which is really just a picture of Christ. I believe Romans 13:14 sums it all up: "Clothe yourselves with the Lord Jesus Christ." In Him, we have all we need, and we *can* be victorious over the attacks of the enemy. I can testify to the truth of that during my forty-two years in Africa!

Battling the Enemy Within
Vicki Fleming
Ministry Wife/Leader

Because I have a vivid imagination, I like to think of my unseen enemies as sinister, creepy-looking villains like extras in a low-budget horror film. Imagine my surprise, then, when the Lord gave me a glimpse of one foul creature, and the face was *mine*!

Supernatural forces can work against anyone in ministry; but I make the job easier for those working against me by just being *me*. The Bible calls this "walking in the flesh." The Lord's road is long yet scenic, and is called "walking in the Spirit." It's long for me because, being rather fond of my flesh walk, I tend to let go of it slowly. It's scenic because the view from the Spirit's road is beautiful though rough, yet God says this way is the only one that leads to spiritual freedom.

As the Lord invites me to move up higher with Him, I see three places where I allow myself to be robbed of the joy of His Spirit: *fear*, which robs me of my peace; *greed*, which robs me of my contentment; and *apathy,* which robs me of my passion.

About facing *fear*, Isaiah 42:16 says, "I will lead the blind by ways they have not known, along unfamiliar paths I will guide them. I will turn the darkness into light before them and make the rough places smooth." When I hear those words, I nod and smile; but when the Lord allows me to walk with Him in the dark I want to tell Him that He's taken the wrong road, as if He doesn't know where we are! I'm afraid that He won't turn the darkness into light and that I'll fall head first down a steep embankment. It's then that fear makes me want to return to something I know; and I freeze, unable to move on with the Lord. Slowly, however, He teaches me to stand, then walk, then even run a little over some very rough ground. Is the road getting smoother? Is He making me more sure-footed? I begin to notice the light that only He can provide, and I see things I couldn't see without Him. Peace replaces fear and I experience real joy.

Then there is *greed*. People in ministry seldom look for greed in their lives. I mean—really? No one makes enough money to buy expensive cars, grand houses, or designer clothes. So what *is* greed? Greed is simply wanting more than we need; and since Philippians 4:19 says that "my God will supply all your needs according to His glorious riches in Christ Jesus" (NASB). I must be wanting that which God has not provided. Ouch! I don't think this means that we must never long to own a home, or that it's wrong to pray that the Lord replaces our rusted-out car, but it is wrong when our desires rob us of contentment. It's greed, then, that tells me I can't be filled with joy because I don't have what I desire.

Finally, it is my *apathy* that robs me of my passion for Jesus Christ. It's not that I don't care. I care a lot; but what I care about can be easily misdirected. When I first came to know Christ's saving love, I wanted to live there forever, enjoying His presence and telling a lost world about Him. I wanted to lay my belongings and family and future on the line for the Gospel. How did it become so easy to trade that passion in for programs? Oh, I still care, but I've calmed down and "matured" and begun a love affair with programs. I spend months planning them—and minutes praying about them. I've learned to perfect programs to meet the needs of the people, but sometimes the programs become the focus while the people become a blur. My love affair with programs is measured by how strongly I feel when someone tries to change them or interrupts the process.

So what am I to do? How do I shed this flesh walk when I've woven it so carefully into my Christianity? I believe that I must go to God's Word, perhaps Psalm 51, and ask the Lord to meet me there. I must ask the Holy Spirit to cut those things out of my life that keep me from walking in the Spirit; and to do it, please, with love and compassion. I must ask Him to "Create in me a clean heart … and renew a steadfast spirit within me" (v.10, NKJV). Only then will the Lord restore the joy of my salvation (see v.12), enabling me to walk in peace, resting in contentment, and finally restoring my passion for Him.

Assault on the Physical
Debbie Fortnum
Pastor's Wife/Worship Leader

When peace like a river attendeth my way,
When sorrows like sea billows roll,
Whatever my lot, Thou hast taught me to say,
"It is well, it is well with my soul."

Early in January 1980, I chose that hymn as my theme song for the new year. Little did I know how the Lord would use it as a means of comfort and as an incentive for trustful surrender for me and my family through the dark and difficult time we were about to face.

Later that month, what at first appeared to be a

mere case of the flu turned out to be the beginning stages of an extremely painful and physically restricting illness that plagued me and perplexed doctors for the next three years.

From the very beginning, my spine and muscles were affected. At times the pain was so intense that my family had to be careful when they hugged me. Within six months my vision deteriorated, and soon I had to use a magnifying glass to read.

Life Lifters

"The one who is in you is greater than the one who is in the world."

—**1 John 4:4**—

Believers from several local congregations held a special time of fasting and prayer for me, but nothing happened. Elders and pastors from different local churches gathered for prayer and anointing. Still nothing. Much prayer was made on my behalf, but there was no physical improvement.

Various specialists and tests in two major hospitals brought us time and again to the same conclusion—nothing. The problem was obvious, but when it came to pinning down the cause, we were batting zero.

I became totally dependent on God's supply of strength and grace which He offered me daily. And then it happened. The songs of worship and praise started to flow out of me. Since I couldn't physically do much more than sit at my piano and sing or read God's Word, I began to develop an incredible intimate relationship with God. My love for Him grew deep as I would prop up my Bible on the piano and literally *sing* the Word and worship Him for hours.

Three years had passed and my condition was worsening. We were encouraged when we were able to enlist the services of a committed Christian doctor. For the very first time in our lives we experienced the support of a medical man who held our hands as he led us in prayer, seeking the wisdom and skill of the Great Physician.

On January 31, 1983, my eyes were tested again. The doctor declared me legally blind. My heart sank!

Shortly afterward, I asked my mother to read to me from Psalm 91. No one knew at the time how beautifully God was preparing my heart for what was to take place later that night. "You will not be afraid of the terror by night, or of ... the pestilence that stalks in darkness ... Because (she) has loved Me, therefore I will deliver (her)," (verses 5-6, 14, NASB).

In the middle of the night, I awakened my mother in fear—something that I had *never* done before. We went back to my room together and prayed. Sometime later, unable to sleep, I began to sense the evil presence of the enemy, and then saw a dark, gray cloud in the corner of my bedroom. Suddenly, an overwhelming sense of faith welled up inside of me, and I sat up in bed and declared in a loud voice, "Satan, in the name of Jesus Christ, I command you to get off my back and stop plaguing me—I am a child of God!" The evil presence promptly left. I began to quietly and joyfully worship the Lord. Then, almost as if a plug was pulled out at the bottom of my feet, I felt the pain literally drain out of my body. For the first time in three years, there was no pain!

Looking back almost eighteen years, I realize that this whole illness started just prior to the missions conference that marked the first anniversary of the call of God on my life to serve Him full time—a fire that continues to burn in my heart as the wife of a senior pastor and a minister of worship. I can well understand the enemy's strategy in attempting to prevent me from following that call. Not only did this painful experience give me a keen sensitivity to the hurts and needs of others, but it also developed the kind of faith that always steers me to the *truth* that even though the enemy always means it for evil, God means it for good. He sees the entire jigsaw while we can only see the one little puzzle piece in our hands! Healing is not everyone's experience, but it was mine. Some have been healed much sooner. Some have waited much longer. Some are still waiting, but through this God has taught me that I exist for His purpose.

If His purpose is facilitated by pain, then pain is a blessed thing. I am convinced that pain became His life-changing tool to sculpt me into the likeness of Jesus. I am also convinced that God used the soil of pain to cultivate lifestyle worship in me. My prayer for us all is that we would be able to accept the words of the hymn writer, "Whatever my lot ... it is well with my soul!"

Bended Knees and Battle Scars
Elizabeth Musser
Missionary Wife

I stared at the thermometer. My two-year-old had a 104-degree fever. Just five minutes earlier, my four-year-old's temperature also had registered 104 degrees. I was used to high fevers, and I knew what to do; but on this Friday morning in March, fevers didn't fit into my schedule.

For months we had been planning and praying for the Billy Graham Crusade that was to take place in Germany. Twelve other European countries would air the event each night via satellite, and our small church in Montpellier, France had worked hard to have all the right equipment.

This weekend was already overflowing with ministry. After each broadcast, my husband and I would be involved in counseling individuals who expressed interest in spiritual matters. Additionally, we had invited different friends throughout the weekend to eat with us and then attend the meetings. These were friends who did not know Jesus; friends for whom we had prayed for years. I thought of all the food I had fixed ahead of time just to be ready for this weekend. Six people were to be at our house tonight and now both boys had high fevers. "What do I do, Lord?"

> ### Life Lifters
>
> "It is startling to think that Satan can actually come into the heart of a man in such close touch with Jesus as Judas was. And more—he is cunningly trying to do it today. Yet he can get in only through a door opened from the inside. 'Every man controls the door of his own life.' Satan can't get in without our help."
>
> —**S. D. Gordon**—

If you've ever found yourself in the middle of a spiritual battle, you'll know I felt the powers of darkness aligned against me. I don't cry "Satan" every time my kids are sick. But that day, with so many prayers and hopes focused on these few nights, I knew the battle was raging around us. The enemy did not want our friends to hear the Gospel.

Relief surged through me as I recalled David facing Goliath against formidable odds, yet remaining steadfast in his faith in God as he proclaimed to the Philistine, "the battle is the Lord's," (1 Sam. 17:47). Then the Lord reminded me of the hundreds of people who were praying for us, specifically interceding for this Crusade. I was greatly encouraged.

Often we are totally unaware of the spiritual warfare that surrounds us. I rarely thought about the spiritual battle affecting me until I became a missionary in France as a young, single woman. But once there, the atmosphere around me and my teammates seemed oppressive and dark. Unexplained occurrences frightened us. Just before we expected six young women for our first Bible study, a window in our apartment broke for no apparent reason. Another time, we screamed in terror as we were awakened in the night by an unearthly, satanic presence hanging over us; and the believers in our tiny church seemed constantly plagued by profound, disturbing problems. We felt homesick and lonely, and depression threatened us. Being new, young missionaries, we felt unprepared for these frightening events.

Then, remembering that the battle was the Lord's, we stood in a circle in each room of each of our apartments and prayed that Jesus' blood would cover our homes and protect us from evil. We prayed every time before we stepped into the open markets to tell of our faith, and we prayed beside the heartbroken brothers and sisters in Christ whose loved ones had been snatched away without warning. When I'd be tempted to think that all we did was pray, the Lord reminded me again and again that prayer was our best defense against the enemy's weapons.

The passage in Ephesians 6 concerning spiritual warfare not only reminds us to put on the full armor of God, but "with all prayer and petition, pray at all times in the Spirit and ... be on the alert with all perseverance and petition for all the saints" (Eph. 6:18, NASB).

It has been said that the best defense is a good offense. When Paul exhorts us to pray at all times in the Spirit, he's reminding me to do likewise as I prepare for whatever ministry I'm involved in. When we pray, we acknowledge our weakness and our dependence on God, realizing that He sees all, knows all, controls all and is never overwhelmed or taken by surprise. What freedom this brings!

Next, we must be aware of the spiritual battle around us. Scripture tells us to be on the alert against Satan's attacks because he knows only too well where our weak spot lies. If we're busy about the Lord's work, perhaps especially in leadership positions, Scripture assures us that he'll take aim and the battle will rage. During those times, however, we should not feel alone, remembering that Jesus is interceding for and along with us, as well as others whom He has prompted also to intercede.

How many times have I stumbled along in the battle, on my own, forgetting to arm myself through prayer? Even now, years after I first stepped onto foreign soil, I sometimes catch myself feeling totally overwhelmed by circumstances, problems, and evil in this world. That's when the Spirit nudges me again to pray. And peace comes back. I remember who is in control. The battle is the Lord's.

I survived that weekend in March. Yes, I was a bit battle-weary and exhausted; but spiritually, God had renewed my strength. We were praying; others were praying; Jesus was interceding. And I remembered who was in control. The battle was indeed the Lord's!

chapter seven

Digging Deeper:
Taking Action
Against the Enemy

Kris Grisa

Though the Scriptures give various faces to the evil one who wars against our souls—a lion, a snake— it's very possible that the face of the most effective warrior against your soul is you.

Two natures struggle within me.
One is cursed, one is blessed.
One I love and one I hate.
The One I feed will eventually dominate.

Meditate on the Following Scripture:

"Search me, O God and know my heart;
Try me and know my anxious thoughts.
And see if there be any hurtful way in me,
And lead me in the everlasting way."
(Ps. 139:23-24, NASB)

Part of winning the battle in spiritual warfare comes through prayer.

The following is an opportunity to dwell prayerfully on your own battlefield:

Jesus, Overcoming One, praise to You for being greater than he who is in the world. Thank You that I have inherited Your power as surely as I have become Your child. Where would I be if I had been left to do battle with the enemy on his terms? Praise to Your infinite goodness! Your Spirit dwells within me, Your fortress surrounds me, Your power is made perfect in my weakness. The jobs You give me to do in this world sometimes frighten me, but I know that You ultimately protect everything I say and do in Your name. I will count on that as if my life depends on it because, indeed, it does.

Jeremiah 1:7-8 says, "But the Lord said to me, 'Do not say, "I am only a child." You must go to everyone I send you to and say whatever I command you. Do not be afraid of them, for I am with you and will rescue you,' declares the Lord."

O Lord, my God, I confess I don't trust my own childish eyes. I see shadows of the lurking enemy lying in wait for me only to find, more often than not, I've feared my own imaginings. In my defense of the Gospel I get mixed up and find I'm caught up in defending myself, and judging someone else's sin. I confess in disgrace that I often discover my own sin is the more fierce of the contenders. I pray for self-control and wisdom to resist sin which is possible only when empowered by Your Spirit. Would You shine Your search light of righteousness on the shadowy areas of my life that I might correctly see what is there? When I fear mere shadows, strengthen my confidence. When the enemy truly advances to devour me, I pray my spiritual armor of truth, righteousness, faith and peace is so indigestible and unpalatable to him that he holds no power to harm. I will not dread the day of unexpected confrontation with him. My focus is on You, Lord; and when I receive a surprising blow from the enemy, I will quickly search for Your arms that pull me to my feet. May a chorus of my supporters—on earth and in heaven—sing songs of victory and rejoicing when the unsuccessful attempts of the enemy lies empty-handed in defeat.

Questions for Personal Evaluation

- Can you recall a time when God pulled you from the mouth of the lion?
- Was your marriage, a child, or a dear friend in danger from spiritual attack?
- Did your lack of faith cloud the victory at any point?
- Thank God for strengthening you.
- Did the prayers of others sweeten the victory as you saw the unity of the body at work?
- Thank God for some of the coworkers He has called onto your battlefield as a way of loving you and ensuring your victory.

Meditate on the Following Passage

Second Corinthians 10:3-5 says, "For though we live in the world, we do not wage war as the world does. The weapons we fight with are not the weapons of the world. On the contrary, they have divine power to demolish strongholds. We demolish arguments and every pretension that sets itself up against the knowledge of God, and we take captive every thought to make it obedient to Christ."

Pray Through the Following Prayer, Making It Your Own

Lord Jesus, I will not shrink back from naming and demolishing the enemies within me who masquerade around, subtly disguised as me. The habits and attitudes of my sinful old nature need nothing more than for me to pretend that I don't recognize them in order to overpower me. Amen.

A Final Inward Look

Are any of these betrayers waltzing freely about your domain because you won't draw the sword of the Spirit against them: bitterness, anger, or unforgiveness? Fear, pride, or independence? Apathy, people pleasing, prejudice? Ingratitude, materialism, or an overburdened spirit?

Disarm the enemy by *confessing* and *kicking the impostors out*. Ask Jesus to continue helping you develop the habits of righteousness that will demolish the attacks of the enemy. Claim His Victory!

chapter eight

Delegate It!

Learn how to give some of your ministry
responsibility away, and watch your ministry grow.

Elizabeth Greene

We've all been there. One look at the schedule and panic sets in as we realize we have so much to do in so little time. The enemy loves for us to become overloaded, thinking we can do it all ourselves. Usually we have one busy season which consumes an even greater amount of time than the regular, ongoing concerns of ministry. My busy season in children's ministry hit during the summer when we sponsored two camps, vacation Bible school, a children's musical, and a family olympics. The demands of the summer pressed in on me as the fall program and recruiting needs loomed on the horizon. I needed to teach, train, provide long-range planning, develop new programs, and lead a staff. How would I get it all done? The task seemed too overwhelming to tackle.

When the weight of ministry wearies our souls, we need to learn the fine art of delegating. Delegating is one practical way to combat spiritual warfare in our ministries, helping us to keep from unnecessarily overloading ourselves, resulting in ineffectiveness for the kingdom. It's been said, "that if the devil can't make us bad, he'll make us busy." That's why the old cliché, "many hands make light work" proves true for those in ministry. We must learn to delegate effectively if we hope to eliminate premature burnout.

> ### Life Lifters
> "*As* we face uncertain spiritual battles ahead often we are not going to know what to do. Remember that the battle is the Lord's. Our job is to turn our gaze upon Him, bow before Him in worshipful trust, wait for His instruction, and wholeheartedly praise Him. He will conquer the enemy and give rest to His people."
> —**Thomas B. White**—

Moses knew the strain of heavy ministry demands. The early chapters of Exodus set the stage for the challenges that lay ahead. After the people left Egypt, they faced many obstacles in the desert. Moses led complaining followers who lacked faith that the God who parted the Red Sea would provide food and water in a barren desert. He played military commander, leader, warrior, and judge.

Perhaps you juggle numerous roles in a multifaceted ministry. You may serve as leader, administrator, counselor, shepherd, and teacher. Perhaps you lead followers who are filled with complaints rather than faith. As you move in and out of your various roles, you must plan wisely so that you will thrive rather than merely survive in the role to which God has called you.

In Exodus 18, Moses' father-in-law, Jethro, came to visit Moses. He saw Moses sitting alone to judge the people and said to him, "What you are doing is not good. You and these people who come to you will only wear yourselves out. The work is too heavy for you; you cannot handle it alone" (Exod. 18:17-18).

Sometimes we glory in "doing it all." We somehow think that our service to the Lord pleases Him more fully when we are functioning in overload, even if we are working inefficiently. Perhaps you need the rebuke of Jethro to challenge your approach to ministry. Jethro counseled Moses to set up a structure so that others would bear the burden with him and he would endure (vv. 22-23). Wisely, Moses listened to his father-in-law and did all that he had said.

We can learn some principles of delegation from this passage. *First*, Jethro told Moses to choose able men. When you have a task to delegate, choose someone who has the skills to do the job. It sounds obvious, but how often do we take the first warm body to fill a need, even if it's a mismatch? I once had a woman who volunteered to write curriculum for our Sunday school program. I desperately needed the help and initially accepted her offer, but later determined her skills didn't match the need. Eventually, I asked her to serve in another area but she clung to the project, which created conflict. Wait for the person with the right skills before delegating the job.

Second, Jethro told Moses to choose men who fear God, men of truth, those who hate dishonest gain. In other words, character counts. Choose people who have a love for God and demonstrate a vibrant relationship with Him. I recently observed a young woman lead a training session for our children's ministry. Her eyes welled up with tears as she spoke of God's goodness in using us to reach kids for the Gospel. Her love for Jesus inspired others to accept the call. Get to know the heart before you hand over responsibility. God looks at the heart and so should we.

Third, delegate rather than dump the job in someone's lap. Provide a structure that will allow a helper to turn to you if they get stuck. Don't leave them to drown in a job that proves too tough for them to handle. Moses allowed his men to settle minor disputes, but the difficult ones Moses resolved. He remained the leader and made the tough calls. Make sure you provide the backup needed for your leaders.

Choose Wisely

You may find the perfect person to lead a program. They have the skills and character, but do they have the time? Don't coax an overcommitted person into taking on further responsibility. At times, I specifically avoid asking my first choice when I know their calendar overflows with prior obligations.

Provide Job Descriptions

Before I delegate a task, I develop a job description. Then I recruit people to fill the roles. People willingly volunteer when they see the requirements on paper, but often quit if the task continues to grow beyond their expectations.

Follow up on Progress

Checkpoints along the way ensure that your volunteer stays on track and enable you to determine progress. A simple phone call or meeting will allow the volunteer to ask questions and enables you to redirect, problem solve, and encourage. You must provide a structure of support for successful delegation. One summer my intern designed some wild games for our Kids Kamp. Meeting together along the way helped me to guide her in designing activities more age appropriate. The final games worked at camp because we met together throughout the process.

Provide Lifelines

On the popular game show, *Who Wants to be a Millionaire?*, a contestant can call a friend when stuck on a question. Ideally, that friend serves as a valuable resource, and the contestant advances in the game. When I sit down with someone taking on a job, I provide a list of resources available to him or her. When people get stuck planning a program, I offer them lifelines. I give them names of people to call, books from my library, or resources to buy at the bookstore. Whatever the need, I try to help them push through their obstacle so they can continue moving forward.

Celebrate a Job Well Done

Everyone loves to hear the words "Well done! I appreciate your hard work and effort. Thank you."

LifeLifters

"*B*e strong in the Lord and in the power of His might. Put on the whole armor of God, that you may be able to stand against the wiles of the devil. For we do not wrestle against flesh and blood, but against principalities, against powers, against the rulers of the darkness of this age, against spiritual hosts of wickedness in the heavenly places. Therefore take up the whole armor of God, that you may be able to withstand in the evil day, and having done all, to stand."

—Ephesians 6:10-13 (NKJV)—

Tell your leaders how God has worked through them to further the kingdom. Be specific in your accolades. Praise them publicly. Write a thank-you note. Share your joy in watching God do great things through the body of Christ. Your leaders will more likely accept future challenges when you celebrate past work.

Ministry can feel less burdensome when you share the load with others. Guard against the two extremes of trying to do it all yourself versus dumping the entire project on someone else and walking away. God has called us to equip the saints for the work of service, to the building up of the body of Christ (Eph. 4:12).

The great joy of delegating is to see the ministry grow well beyond you as you equip others for service. Several years ago, I started an inductive Bible study group for fourth and fifth grade girls. I pulled other leaders into the process of leading and teaching the study. The next year the group doubled in size and we added new leaders. When the time came for me to step away from the program, it continued to flourish because able men and women had gained the skills and vision to carry on the work. What a joy to see the work grow beyond me. Delegating will take you down the path of growing the ministry and enduring long term. It will also keep you from falling into the enemy's trap of trying to do it all, which can lead to burnout and joylessness in ministry. May your ministry bear fruit as you develop the fine art of delegating.

chapter nine

Counseling Corner:
Women in Ministry
Need Boundaries Too

Ingrid Lawrenz, MSW

*J*enny had a difficult Wednesday. She had spent four hours at a music seminar with her husband, Tim, a youth pastor. She wasn't interested in music but didn't want to hurt his feelings. Later, when she met a friend from church for coffee, she needed to vent. Like an open faucet she lamented her husband's indifference to her and his impulsive spending of money on another new guitar.

In the evening, she juggled which late bills to pay while cooking supper and listening to her kids' accounts of their school day. Her pleas to help set the table and pick up the family room were drowned out by the volume of the cartoons on TV. After dinner, Jenny was rushing to get out the door when her mother called to tell her about her sister's marital problems. Unable to shorten the call, she was now late for her study group on *Spiritual Disciplines* (a subject she co-led but rarely had time to practice because of her busyness).

During the study Jenny was convinced several of the ladies didn't like her because they didn't include her in their small talk. So Jenny tried extra hard to be nice to them. She felt she had made some progress because before she left one of the ladies told her she needed to look more professional and offered to pay for Jenny to have her hair done.

Do you sympathize with Jenny? She appears to be trying so hard. Yet Jenny has major problems with boundaries, and she allowed the enemy to gain a foothold in her life by trying to be all things to all people—one of Satan's subtlest tactics, by the way. Women in ministry, especially, need to have clear and well-thought-out boundaries because, if they don't, the enemy can very slyly sneak in and confuse their priorities and purpose. A perennial question I hear is, "Can you be friends with people in your congregation?" While there is no black or white answer to this, the best answer is, "Yes, but with good boundaries."

In the scenario described above, Jenny was not being honest with herself or setting appropriate boundaries. She was allowing other people to tell her what to do, what to like, and how to look, a common trap of Satan. She may have been so used to focusing on others that she no longer even knew the truth about what her true feelings, opinions, and thoughts were. Like many others with diffuse boundaries, she didn't respect or uphold others' boundaries either. She spoke ill of her husband, she was late, and she enabled her kids to be irresponsible, thus making her ineffective.

Here are some suggested boundaries that I have gleaned from the wisdom of many ministry wives. I have found it helpful to think in terms of boundaries around issues not people. Also, before speaking, assume what you say probably will get broadcast to others! Then

Subjects Best Kept Confidential

- Salary and major spending decisions
- Marital problems
- Spouse's past or present failings
- Confidential counseling issues of parishioners
- Internal church problems or conflicts
- Personal prayer requests from parishioners
- Staff members' conflicts or problems
- Personal sin areas that would hurt your spouse's ministry or your own ministry—temptations to have an affair, for instance. However, it is vitally important to share this with a mentor!

make a decision about what is safe to share.

For example, for me personally, things I could readily share with church friends would include my journey of faith, parenting issues, my love of animals, my limitations with cooking, my struggles with infertility, growing up in an alcoholic home, and migraines. Even in this incomplete list there is certainly enough for a wide range of deep and meaningful friendships.

It is vital, however, to have one or more confidantes outside of your congregation—friends from out of town, a supervisor, mentor, or your own counselor. We all need places where we can turn for help, clarity, and accountability.

A final aspect of boundaries that ministry women need to remember is that while we are asked to

---

Subjects Appropriate to Share

- Service projects
- Hobbies
- Sports
- Health subjects
- Movies, books
- Current events
- Cooking and home decorating
- Educational issues
- Background stories
- Interests
- Prayer requests
- Fun family activities
- Parenting issues (with discernment)
- Personal struggles (with discernment)

"mourn with those who mourn and rejoice with those who rejoice," we are not responsible for other people's pain. We are not responsible for other people's choices, and we are not responsible for how others treat others. We can come alongside someone, but we can't suffer for someone. We hear so much about pain, hurt, betrayal, and anguish that it can feel as though it is our own suffering. We need to remind ourselves of setting realistic boundaries so we don't burn out, which is what the enemy desires, and we need to be able to let go and focus on what God has put on our own plate.

For a more detailed discussion of boundaries, several excellent resources are *Boundaries, Boundaries in Marriage*, and *Boundaries with Kids* by Dr. Henry Cloud and Dr. John Townsend.

Author Biographies

Jill Briscoe is a popular writer and conference speaker who has authored over forty books. She directs Telling the Truth media ministries with her husband, Stuart, and ministers through speaking engagements around the world. Jill is executive editor of *Just Between Us*, a magazine for ministry wives and women in leadership, and serves on the boards of World Relief and Christianity Today International. Jill and Stuart live in suburban Milwaukee, Wisconsin, and have three grown children and thirteen grandchildren.

Stuart Briscoe, a native of England, has served as senior pastor of Elmbrook Church in Brookfield Wisconsin, for the last thirty years. Stuart recently stepped down to become a minister-at-large along with his wife, Jill, so they can focus more of their time ministering to pastors and missionaries overseas. He has preached in more than one hundred countries. He and his wife have three grown children and 13 grandchildren and reside in suburban Milwaukee, Wisconsin.

Patty Stump is a frequent speaker at women's retreats and special events across the country. Patty is also a Bible study leader, a contributing writer to over 14 books, and a workshop leader at the Billy Graham Training Center at The Cove in Asheville, North Carolina. She and her husband, Ted, have two children and live in Montreat, North Carolina.

Shelly Esser has bee the editor of *Just Between Us*, a magazine for ministry wives and women in leadership, for the last thirteen years. She has written numerous published articles and ministered to women for over twenty years. Her recent book, *My Cup Overflows—A Deeper Study of Psalm 23* encourages women to discover God's shepherd love and care for them. She lives in southeastern Wisconsin, with her husband, John, and four daughters.

Jean Robinson spent forty-two years in Africa as a missionary to Zaire. After serving for the last fifteen years on the staff of Elmbrook Church in Brookfield, Wisconsin, she retired to Clermont, Florida to her mission retirement center. Jean has also been the correspondent editor for Just Between Us, a magazine for ministry wives and women in leadership. Throughout her life, Jean has used her teaching gifts extensively through various women's programs, adult Sunday school, and outside speaking engagements.

Vicki Fleming and her husband, Jim, are on staff at Fort Wilderness, an exciting camping ministry in Northern Wisconsin. Vicki mentors high school and college-aged staff at "The Fort," directs drama and worship teams, and is a popular keynote speaker for college and women's groups throughout the Midwest. She has two teenagers and lives in Lake Tomahawk, Wisconsin.

Debbie Fortnum is a pastor's wife, worship leader, recording artist, and songwriter with Canadian Food for the Hungry International, and the director of women's ministries at Yarrow Alliance Church in British Columbia. Her life has been marked by many seasons of pain. She ministers abroad with her Scripture-based music, sharing the message of hope and healing. She and her husband have three children and live in Sardis, B.C., Canada.

Elizabeth Musser has been involved for the last 15 years with her husband, Paul, in mission work with International Teams. For the past thirteen years, Elizabeth has lived in Montpellier, France where they are church planters. Elizabeth is involved in women's ministries, evangelism, discipleship and youth work. Additionally, Elizabeth has authored four novels and has been a writer for *Just Between Us*, the magazine for ministry wives and women in leadership. She has two sons.

Kris Grisa has spent many years involved in small group leadership. She is an avid disciple maker, teaching women and girls in small group settings through her local church. Kris is also a writer of devotional materials. She and her husband, John, live in Brookfield, Wisconsin, with their three children.

Elizabeth Greene has an M.A. in Christian Education and formerly served as a children's ministry pastor for six years at Elmbrook Church in Brookfield, Wisconsin. Elizabeth continues to remain active in children's and women's ministries through teaching and speaking. She lives in Waukesha, Wisconsin, with her husband, Ryan, and two children.

Ingrid Lawrenz, MSW is a licensed social worker who has been counseling for seventeen years. Ingrid has been a pastor's wife for twenty-seven years and is currently the senior pastor's wife at Elmbrook Church in suburban Brookfield, Wisconsin. She and her husband, Mel, have two teenagers and live in Waukesha, Wisconsin.

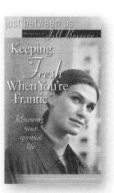

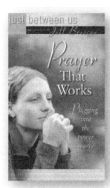

Prayer that Works
Plugging into the
power source.
ISBN 0-78143-953-1
ITEM #102352

Only
$5.99
each!

Resolving Conflict
Stilling the storms of life.
ISBN 0-78143-954-X
ITEM #102353

The Search for Balance
Keeping first things first.
ISBN 0-78143-955-8
ITEM #102354

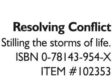

Spiritual Warfare
Equipping yourself for battle.
ISBN 0-78143-948-5
ITEM #102347